# Majestic

Original Text and Photography

by

Roger D. King

Copyright ©Roger D. King

Affirmation Media, LLC

All rights reserved.

ISBN-13: 978-1984926654

ISBN-10: 1984926659

## ACKNOWLEDGMENTS

Special Thanks to the following:

Terry B. King, Joyce Glass The Write Coach, Brian and Lisa McNeill of Empowerment Media and Publishing, Colleen Wietmarschen and Peter Wietmarschen of Your Literary Prose, Natasha Bachar, Donna Taylor and "Awesome Angie" Engstrom for all of your encouragement.

And a HUGE thank you to my editor, Bonnie Jean Alford of Alford Enterprises.

I praise God Almighty for the gift's and talents that He has blessed me with.

## Why This Book?

The original title of this book "Today's Prayer Points" was the result of periodic Facebook Postings that we decided to compile and create a book. The current title, "Majestic" is the result of an encouraging comment regarding my photography made by Lisa Santiago McNeill.

Prayer is one of the key practices of a Believer's life. Often, we are too busy to take time to pray. God is not concerned about the amount of time that we spend in prayer, but THAT we pray.

Sometimes prayer is only one word, one sentence, or a silent cry. The purpose of this small book is to provide a simple prayer guide that can be used anywhere, anytime. There is no set pattern or guideline to using the book. Just use it. It's simple, practical, and easy to read. While you are at it, please take time to enjoy the Majestic Images that are also included in this volume.

Space is left intentionally for you to write your thoughts and/or your own prayers.

May it encourage you to take time to pray, and develop a life of prayer, even if you feel you are too busy to pray.

Rest in HIM and His Majesty.
†
Blessings,

Roger D. King, Visionary

**Faith**

Heavenly Father

Thank You for YOUR grace and mercy over my life. Without it, I would be without hope. Help me to remain focused on The Hope that is only found in Your Son Jesus. May my Faith TRULY be the "substance" of what I HOPE for, and a reflection of the "evidence" of things not seen, that which YOU have in store for the future. Help me to continue to constantly look to and for YOUR help in all that I do in order to obey and please You in and by Faith. I Thank You for being The Rewarder.

In Jesus' Name, Amen†

Hebrews 11:1-6

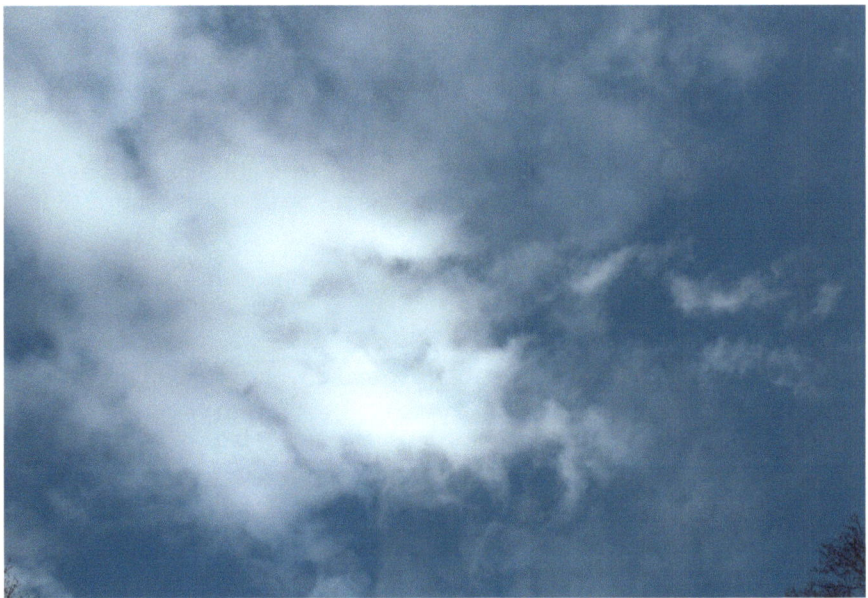

**Son of God**

Heavenly Father

Thank You for loving US so much that You sent "This MAN, Jesus The Christ", YOUR Son into the world. You sent Him to save and deliver us from the penalty that is required for our sins. None of us are exempt from that penalty, except through and by "This MAN, Jesus The Christ." Father, give us understanding of YOUR love for us, and the grace that You have freely given to us. May those who are not currently serving or know You come to Know You.

May those who are serving and worshipping other gods, as well as those who do not know of You, come to Know You RIGHT NOW, in The Mighty Name of Jesus. May those of us who have come to the Saving Knowledge of Him continue to live a life that is pleasing in Your eyes. May we continue to take a stand for You, and Your Word. May we all come to know You more and more in order to worship You in Spirit and In Truth.
In Jesus' Name, Amen†

"But this man, after he had offered one sacrifice for sins forever, sat down on the right hand of God."
Hebrews 10:12

**Purpose**

Heavenly Father

Help us to know and understand "The Works" that YOU have called us to, "The Works" that YOU have given us to perform. Help us to do "The Work" willingly without hesitation or remorse. Help us to focus on YOU for our strength and understanding for "The Work" at hand. Help us Father to work together in unity, peace, and love according to YOUR will, plan, and way. Father, may those who come into contact with us see Your Son Jesus IN US. Help us to stand bold, strong, and faithful in The Calling and Work that YOU have assigned us to do.
In Jesus' Mighty Name, amen†

**27.** "Do not work for the food which perishes, but for the food which endures to eternal life, which the Son of Man will give to you, for on Him the Father, God, has set His seal." **28.** Therefore they said to Him, "What shall we do, so that we may work the works of God?" **29.** Jesus answered and said to them, "This is the work of God, that you believe in Him whom He has sent."
John 6:27-29

## Wisdom

Heavenly Father

Today we ask nothing of You except YOUR Wisdom. We repent for being lazy, slothful, and disobedient. We repent for our lack of time in prayer, our lack of time with Your Word, our lack of time in Your Presence. Father forgive us for not taking a righteous stand against sin and evil. Forgive us Father for being silent when we should be speaking and speaking when we should be silent.
Lord, give us WISDOM.

Give us Wisdom in our times of doubt and confusion. Father, Grant us Wisdom. Lord, YOUR WISDOM. With Your Wisdom, Father, we will know HOW to pray, HOW to love one another, HOW to serve, and HOW take a stand. With Your Wisdom, we become bold, with a Holy Boldness, empowered by You, the Holy Spirit. We thank You Father for hearing us as we seek You for Wisdom.

In Jesus' Name, amen †

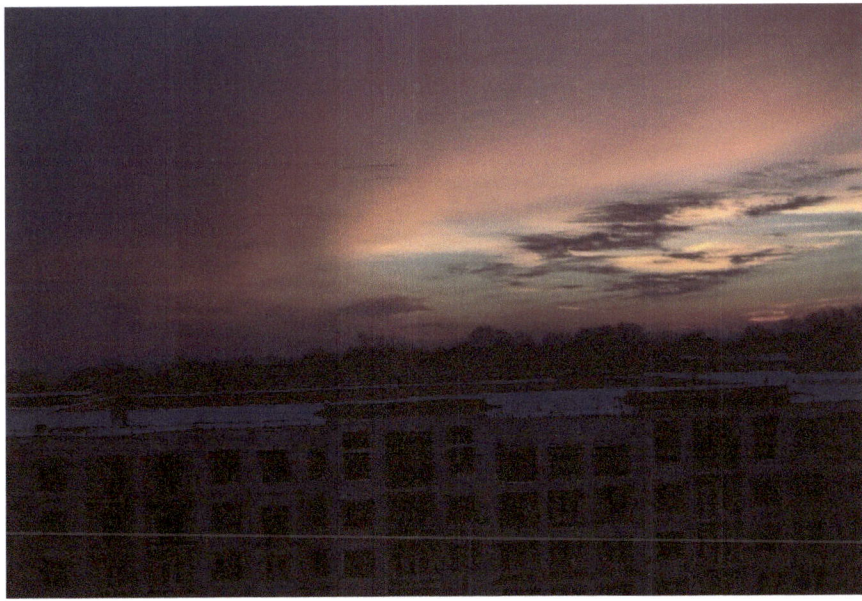

## Humility

Jumping to conclusions. Have you ever found yourself in a situation that you were in control of? Or, at least you felt that you were? Too often we find ourselves in the middle of a problem because we did not take time to stop, listen, and think before responding by "jumping to a conclusion." And in most cases, the wrong conclusion. Well, let us take the time to THINK about the "conclusion of a matter" before responding. It will save a whole lot of unnecessary stress and frustration.
Heavenly Father

Help me today to take time to stop, listen, and think BEFORE I respond to anyone. You are a Father of Love and Grace and because of that Love and Grace, I can run to YOU for help. Help in every area of my life, especially my soul (mind, will, and emotions). Help me to give up my need to always be right and to develop the skill of being a better listener.

Father

Help me to focus on what truly matters most in all things. The one conclusion that matters most is having proper respect for You and your commandments, your instructions; which is MY duty, my responsibility and is the "conclusion whole of the matter."
In Jesus' Name, Amen†

Ecclesiastes 12:13-14

**Gifts and Talents**

Everything and everyone has a purpose, yet we often overlook our own God-given purpose. We overlook our gifts and talents that have been given to us. Most often, our true purpose can be found in our gifts and talents. In some cases, our purpose is discovered as a result of our desire to improve and use our gifts and talents.

Do not hide, or bury, what God has graced you with. Do not neglect the natural AND spiritual gifts and talents that God has blessed you with. Let's NOT try to be so deep and impressive that we mislead people in who we truly are and what we stand for or are trying to achieve. Use YOUR gifts and talents to lift someone else up, even as you are taking care of your "house."

Place God FIRST in everything You do because HE is the one that has blessed you and I with concepts, ideas, and plans. HE is THE ONE who provides the answer we need.

## Honoring God

Heavenly Father

Today, I decide to make YOU my priority.
I place YOU first in my life and turn over all of my plans and ideas to YOU.

Heavenly Father

YOU blessed me with natural abilities in order to provide for my family, as well as to be a blessing to others. Help me to NOT waste what You have blessed me with by hiding and burying the gifts and talents that You have instilled in me. Help me to use everything You have given me for YOUR Glory.

Lord, help me to remain humble as You bless me and raise me to new heights in You. Give me wisdom, courage, and patience as I take each step towards the goals, dreams, and visions that You have inspired me with. Even if it means giving up some things, some people, or dreams that I have, in order for me to be in YOUR perfect will.

Lord put me where YOU want me to be. I ask You for guidance, wisdom, and understanding.

In Jesus' Name, Amen†

Proverbs 16:1-33

**Armor of God**

Heavenly Father

Thank YOU for a brand-new day. A day that for some will never be seen. Some may even not see the end of today. Help me Father to focus on what truly matters most. Help me to put aside the pettiness of worry, and to put on "the armor" that YOU provided me. Help me to fulfill YOUR purpose for me and to lay aside my passion for Yours.
In Jesus' Name, Amen†

Ephesians 6:11

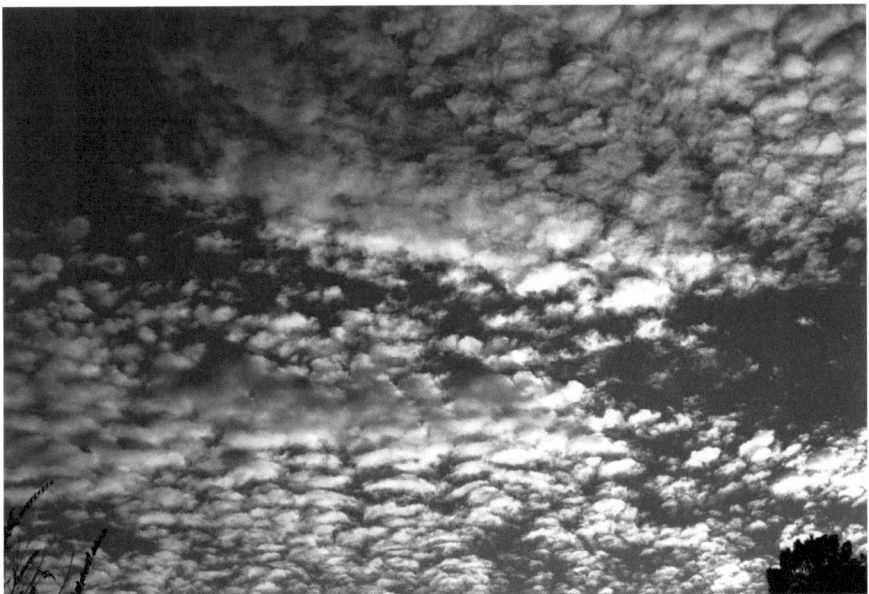

**Determination**

Heavenly Father

I ask for Wisdom and Understanding for the things I have to accomplish today. Help me to remain focused, and intent on meeting the goals and competing my tasks.

In Jesus' Name, Amen†

**God's Promises**

Heavenly Father

Thank You for the promises that are found in Your Word. Please help me to search, find, and accept those promises. Help me to work hard at finding the promises that apply to my life. Help me to be an encouragement to someone else who is struggling with their promises by being an example that brings You glory.

Lord, Your glory is being revealed all around us. Help us to see it. Help us to reflect it. Help us to live it.

Heavenly Father

Even though I believe and know that You have already worked out everything for my good, help me to TRULY believe without doubting. Without being fearful. Without compromise. Without being double-minded.

Heavenly Father

For those who do not have a relationship with You, I pray that today becomes the day that changes for them.
In Jesus' Name, Amen†

"Lord I Believe, but please, HELP My Unbelief."
Mark 9:24

## Wisdom

We thank You, Father, for hearing us as we seek You for Wisdom.
In Jesus' Name, Amen†

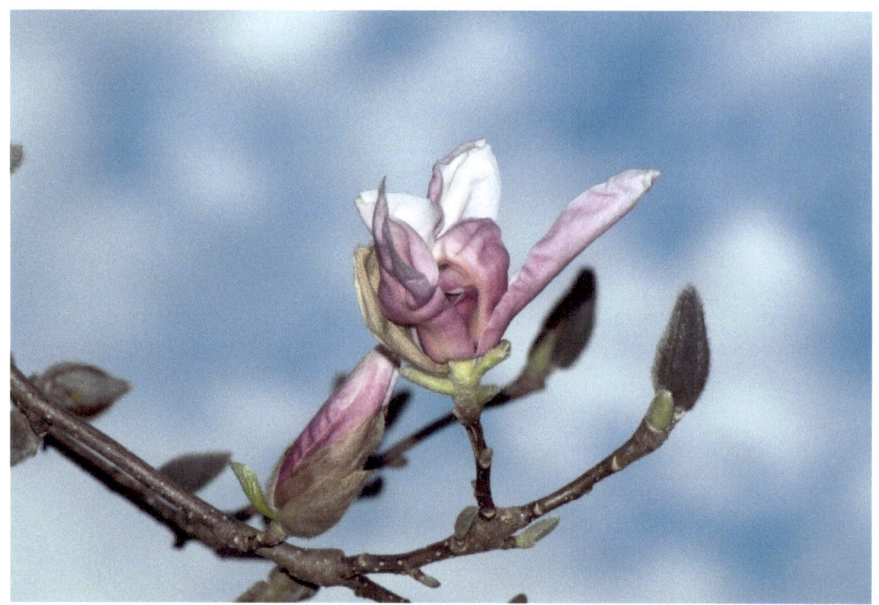

**Insight**

Heavenly Father

Reveal to me today who my "true" friends are. Those who are not out to manipulate me into bad situations and circumstances.

Make me into a true friend to others in order to show your grace, mercy, and love. Help me to follow the example of my True Friend, Your Son, Christ Jesus. Give me insight and clarity of vision to see what I need to see and to be who I need to be, for Your Glory.

In Jesus' Name, Amen†

## Service

Heavenly Father

Thank YOU for a brand-new day. A day never seen before. Help me to use YOUR gift of time wisely, help me to reflect YOUR light, YOUR love, YOUR grace, and YOUR power!

Give me wisdom for today's transactions and tasks. Give me strength to serve.

Grant me YOUR humility for correction.

In Jesus' Name, Amen✝

**Peace**

Dear Lord, give me PEACE.

In Jesus' Name, Amen†

**Thank You**

Heavenly Father

Thank You.
Thank you for your protection, your grace and your mercy upon my life.

In Jesus' Name, Amen†

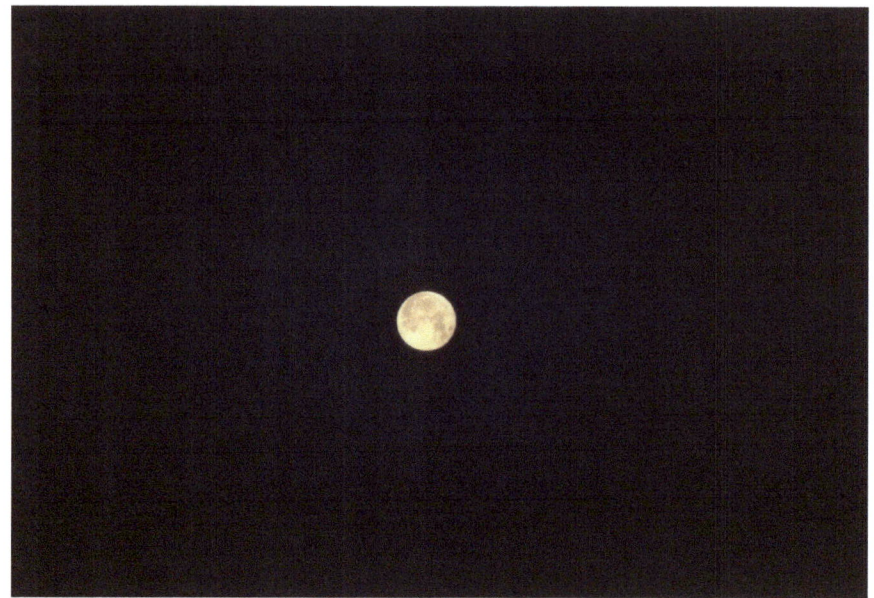

**Trust**

Heavenly Father

Help me to put and KEEP my trust in YOU, and NOT in myself. Help me to make Your Word My priority and not my secondary option. Help me to ALWAYS be thankful in all things according to Your Word.

In Jesus' Name, Amen✝

**Calm**

Heavenly Father

Calm every storm in my life.

In Jesus' Name, Amen†

Psalm 34

**Boldness in Truth**

Heavenly Father

We pray for those who are serving as YOUR Ministers, Your servants. Those whom You have called and chosen for the amazing task of sharing showing and proclaiming the Love of Jesus. That Jesus, YOUR beloved Son, has already Won the Victory over sin, death, hell, and the grave on our behalf.

We pray that Your servants continue to proclaim the truth from Your Word. To promote unity among the saint and to bring YOU glory. Staying away from made up stories, fables, and myths that go against Your Word. To proclaim healing, deliverance, and salvation to all who are bound.

Heavenly Father

May Your Word become our priority and our passion.

In Jesus' Mighty Name, Amen†

2 Peter 1

**Love**

Father, let others see The LOVE of Jesus IN and THROUGH me.

In Jesus' Name, Amen✝

**How to Pray**

Heavenly Father

I ask for clear understanding of HOW to Pray and WHAT to pray. Help me to hear YOUR words regarding prayer in a way that moves me to Pray more effectively, not only for myself, but for others.

Help to not repeat Your words as great quotes and clichés, but to repeat Your words in FAITH, believing YOU for the answer, clear direction, and pure understanding.

Help me to understand what it truly means to humble myself and pray, to seek Your Face. Show me any wicked ways that I have not turned from and forgive me and heal "my land."

Thank You, Heavenly Father, for hearing my prayer.

In Jesus' Name, Amen†

"If my people, which are called by my name, shall humble themselves, and pray, and seek my face, and turn from their wicked ways; then will I hear from heaven, and will forgive their sin, and will heal their land."
2 Chronicles 7:14

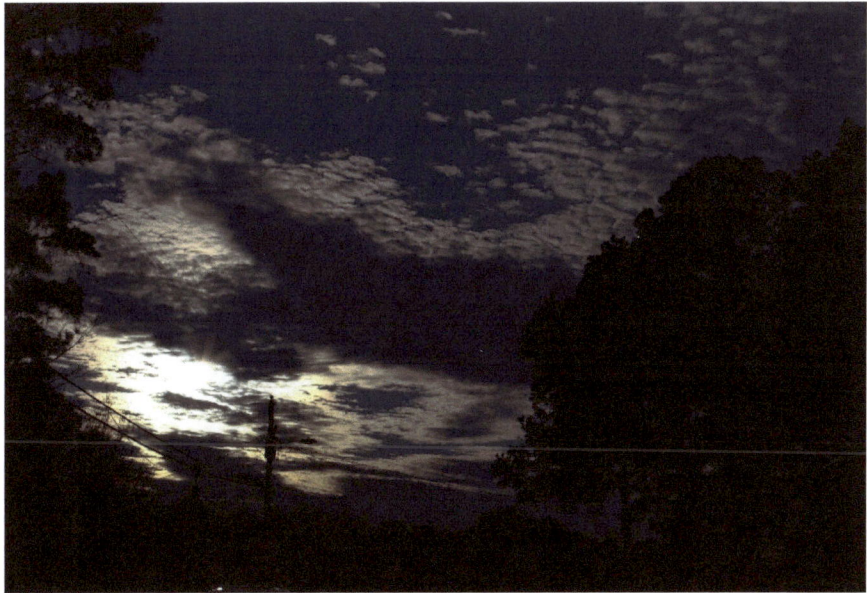

**Why?**

Heavenly Father

Help us all to see that YOU and ONLY YOU have ALL of The answers as to "WHY."

In Jesus' Name, Amen†

**You Have Control, Lord**

Lord

Help ME to "take my hands off" so that YOU have total control, in EVERY area of my life.

In Jesus' Name, Amen†

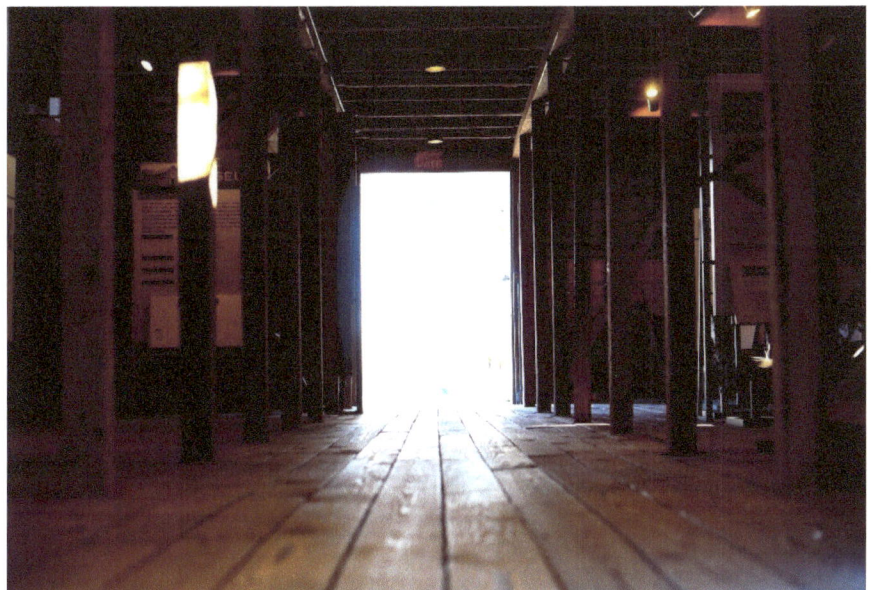

**Your Wisdom**

Heavenly Father

May Your wisdom become my understanding, so that all things You lead me to will be clear and unhindered by the enemy.

In Jesus' Name, Amen†

**Action**

Father

Thank you for all You have done, are doing, and will do IN me and THROUGH me, according to Your Word.

In Jesus' Name, Amen✝

**Honor**

Father in Heaven

May my testimony regarding your goodness to me bring glory, honor, and praise to You.

In Jesus' Name, Amen†

**Not My Will**

Heavenly Father

Not MY will, or the will of anyONE else, BUT YOUR WILL. May it be done in My life.

In Jesus' Name, Amen†

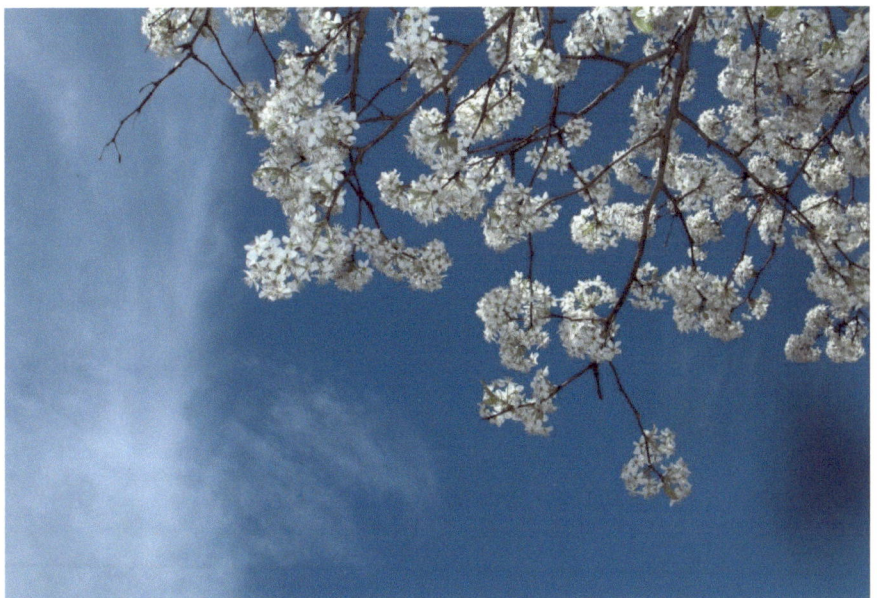

**Priority**

Lord

May I continue to keep YOU as the number one desire and priority in my life.

In Jesus' Name, Amen✝

**God Loves ME in Spite of Me**

Heavenly Father

Thank You for loving me in spite of me. Thank you for always being there for me during the toughest times of my life. Even when I did not look to you, you still Loved me.

Even when I missed the mark and sinned against You, you still Loved me. When those whom I thought were my friends and loved ones turned against me, You still Loved me. No matter what troubles came my way, You were always there WITH me and FOR me.

I am thankful for Your Love for me. Help me to always remember that You Loved me before You even created me.
Thank You, Father.

In Jesus' Name, Amen†

"I will rejoice and be glad in Your faithful love because You have seen my affliction. You have known the troubles of my life."
Psalm 31:7

**Storm of Life**

Heavenly Father

In this world of chaos and darkness, may The Light of Your Glory shine through, so that Jesus is seen and not me.

I pray that any and every "storm" assigned to bring destruction to me and my family be dissolved NOW.

In Jesus' Name, Amen†

Psalm 91

**Provision**

Heavenly Father

Thank you for providing the means and the way for us to hear and/or to read words of wisdom, words of counsel, and words of correction. Help us to receive each as needed for our own lives.

Help us to not become arrogant and high-minded as if we are exempt from counsel and/or correction. Lead and guide us into ALL truth by Your Spirit. Help us to walk and live in Unity, Peace, and Love, and to place a HIGHER Priority on You and YOUR Word. May our boasting always be about You.

In Jesus' Name, Amen†

"My brothers and sisters, rejoice in the Lord. To write the same things to you, to me indeed is not grievous, but for you it is safe."
Philippians 3:1

## Protection and Guidance

Heavenly Father

Thank you in advance for Your protection and guidance for today.
Help me to be productive and not lose focus on what You have given me to do. Give me peace, joy, holy boldness, and The Love of Jesus to deal with any hindrance, to stand against the evil one, to always give You Glory.

I pray for those who are sick, and in need of healing. I pray for those who are bound, in need of deliverance. I pray for those who are lost, that they be found, and led to Christ Jesus.

I Thank You, Father, and Praise You for Who You Are.

In Jesus' Name, Amen†

## Let Your Glory Rise

Lord

Let Your glory rise and shine in me and through me, for YOUR glory and not my own.

In Jesus' Name, Amen†

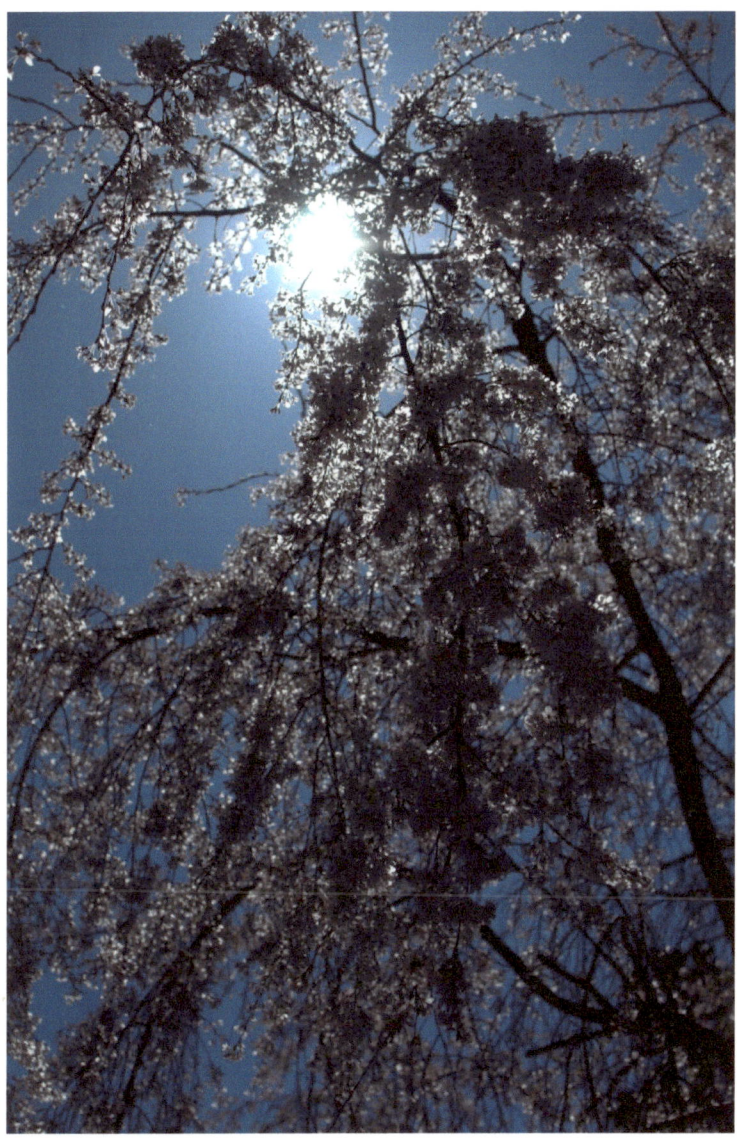

## The Gift of Wisdom

Father

Give us wisdom, Your wisdom for every area of our lives in order to glorify You.

In Jesus' Name, Amen†

**Forgive**

Be honest enough WITH YOURSELF and YOUR LOVED ONEs when YOU have missed it. Frustration leads to aggravation, which hinders your focus along with your progress. Once you take a good look at the situation you will realize an enormous amount of time and energy has been wasted. In most cases, it's REALLY not THAT serious after all.

Heavenly Father

Forgive us for not taking responsibility for our words, actions, and thoughts. If our mind is NOT focused on YOU and YOUR word, we are NOT in the right standing. Forgive us for complaining and focusing on our selfishness, rather than focusing on YOU, YOUR Grace, YOUR Mercy, and YOUR Love, that we SHOULD be showing and sharing to, with, and for others, especially those who are in our own household.
Thank You, Father, for a Fresh Start, and a Brand-New Day.

In Jesus' Name, Amen†

Romans 8:1-39

**Prayer of Deliverance**

Heavenly Father

Deliver me from all unrighteousness and sin. Deliver me from the things that keep me from You and Your Word. Deliver me from the bad situations that I willingly or unwillingly have gotten myself into. Deliver me from financial debt, which is a type of bondage. Deliver me from all evil spirits that hinder me. Deliver me from all guilt and shame.

Give me the strength, boldness, and freedom that can only be found In You through Christ Jesus. Thank You for being my place of safety and my protector! Thank you for redeeming me by The Blood of The Lamb. Thank You, Father, for hearing my prayer and helping me to remain focused and committed to You, Your Word, and All Your Ways.
In Jesus' Name, Amen†

"In You, O LORD, I put my trust; Let me never be ashamed; Deliver me in Your righteousness. Bow down Your ear to me. Deliver me speedily; Be my rock of refuge, A fortress of defense to save me. For You are my rock and my fortress; Therefore, for Your name's sake, Lead me and guide me. Pull me out of the net which they have secretly laid for me, For You are my strength. Into Your hand I commit my spirit; You have redeemed me, O LORD God of truth."
Psalm 31:1-5

**My Safe Place**

Heavenly Father

As we start our day, help us to keep our focus on You. Help us to be reminded throughout the day that our place of safety is in You, because of You. Help us to always have our faith and trust in You, for everything concerning us.

Thank You, Father, for being our place of safety, our defender; The One we can trust in.

In Jesus' Name, Amen†

"I will say of the LORD, He is my refuge and my fortress: my God; in him will I trust."
Psalm 91:2

**Focus**

Heavenly Father

Please reveal YOUR purpose and plan more clearly, so that I will understand it without doubting. Help me to focus on what YOU have ordained for me to do for YOU with, and in my life. Help me to see truth, purity. and righteousness according to YOUR word. Help me to NOT be one who strives "fits in with the crowd" for the sake of having friends and associates, but to be one who is striving to please and obey YOU.

Heavenly Father

Help us to not become distracted and discouraged in serving You. Help us to keep our focus and faith in YOU. Father, let us not be found wandering away from you for any reason. YOU know our hearts, and YOU know what we are going to do before we do, so Lord we ask for YOUR wisdom and YOUR guidance in EVERY area of our life. Father help us to remember by example of Your disciples that we will be tempted to give up and quit. That we can be zealous and on fire for You, yet can still fall short of YOUR glory. May that NOT be the case with us today.

Empower us by Your Spirit to be faithful to YOU and to Your Word in all that we do. May our life bring glory and honor to You.

In Jesus' Name, Amen†

26 "And when they had sung an hymn, they went out into the mount of Olives." 27 "And Jesus said to them, All ye shall be offended because of me this night: for it is written, I will smite the shepherd, and the sheep shall be scattered." 28 "But after that I am risen, I will go before you into Galilee." 29 "But Peter said unto him, Although all shall be offended, yet will not I."
30 "And Jesus said to him, Verily I say to you, That this day, even in this night, before the cock crow twice, you shalt deny me thrice (three times)." 31 "But Peter spoke the more vehemently, If I should die with you, I will not deny you in any wise. Likewise also said they all."
Mark 14:26-31

**Whom Shall I Fear?**

1 "THE LORD is my light and my salvation; whom shall I fear? the LORD is the strength of my life; of whom shall I be afraid?" 2 "When the wicked, even mine enemies and my foes, came upon me to eat up my flesh, they stumbled and fell."

3 "Though an host should encamp against me, my heart shall not fear: though war should rise against me, in this will I be confident." 4 "One thing have I desired of the LORD, that will I seek after; that I may dwell in the house of the LORD all the days of my life, to behold the beauty of the LORD, and to enquire in his temple."

5 "For in the time of trouble he shall hide me in his pavilion: in the secret of his tabernacle shall he hide me; he shall set me up upon a rock."
6 "And now shall mine head be lifted up above mine enemies round about me: therefore will I offer in his tabernacle sacrifices of joy; I will sing, yea, I will sing praises unto The LORD."

Psalm 27:1-6

**Humility**

Heavenly Father

Help us to remain meek and humble in Your sight, according to Your Word. Help us to never become self-righteous. Teach us how to be confident and assured IN YOU, and not in our own thinking and ways.

Forgive us for our self-righteous attitude that subtly demeans others. Forgive us for not putting YOU and Your Word first and foremost. The opinions of others do not matter, what matters in what YOU say.

Help us, help ME, to always walk in Love, and Humility even when we are wrong. Without You, without YOUR Help, it cannot be done. Thank You Father for YOU Loving Kindness and Your Peace.

In Jesus' Name, Amen†
Psalm 51
Romans 3:10
Matthew 23
Romans 2:17-24

**Seasons**

Heavenly Father

Thank You for This New Beginning. Help us to remember your promise to us that "as long as the earth remains, seedtime and harvest, cold and heat, summer and winter, day and night" will continue.

Help us to recognize that season's change and repeat over and over. Help us to recognize the "season" that we are in, and that YOU have our best interest in Mind. Help us to properly prepare for FUTURE seasons to come so that we are able to be examples and encouragement to and for others who are struggling through whatever season they find that they are in.

In Jesus' Name, Amen†

Genesis 8:22
Jeremiah 29:11
Romans 8

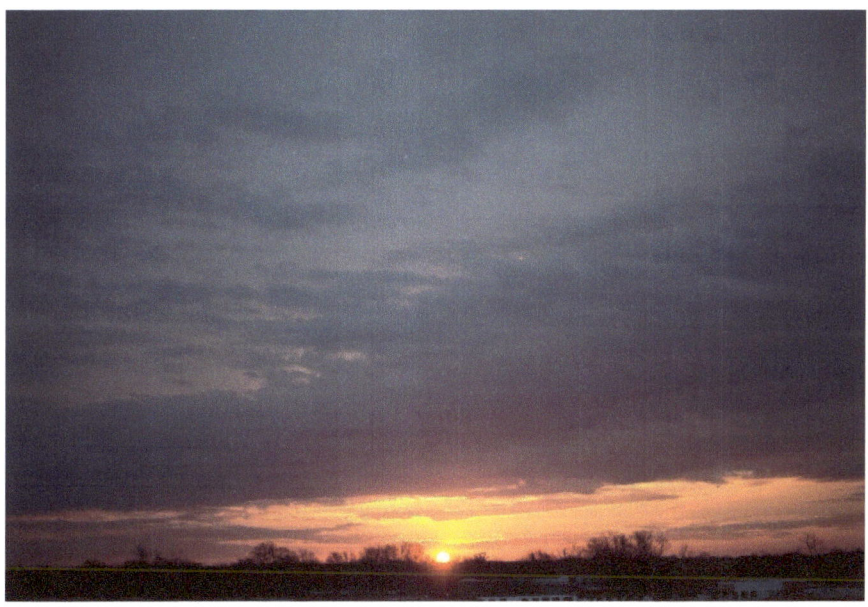

**Shalom (Peace)**

Heavenly Father

Thank YOU for not giving up on us as Your creation. We are becoming hardened and loveless, selfish and stingy. We are becoming elitist and clique-minded. We are becoming everything that You have warned us NOT to become, YET, you are STILL giving us a chance to change.

Thank You for an opportunity to TRY again, to GET BACK UP, and to enjoy The Blessings of Life, Love, Peace, and Unity. Thank YOU for YOUR grace and mercy Through Christ Jesus, THE One Who paid the Ultimate Price for THE WHOLE WORLD, and that includes ME.

Thank You Jesus. May Jesus Be THE Peace today and forever.

In Jesus' Name, Amen†

**Glory**

Heavenly Father

Help us to always be ready to help others who are in need. Help us NOT to look down on others who are hurting and hopeless. May The Light of Jesus shine brightly through US in order to give glory and honor to You, To bring glory and honor to Jesus through and by The Power of Your Spirit living IN Us.

May we always be led by Holy Spirit to do what is just and pleasing and right, according to Your Word, Your Will, and Your Way.

In Jesus' Name, Amen†

**Seeking HIM**

Heavenly Father

Help us to TRULY seek YOU because of WHO you ARE and not because of WHAT you can do for us. May our SEEKING You be with pure motives and intent, to Obey You, to Worship You, In Spirit AND in TRUTH.

Thank You for changing what needs to be changed in US, making us people who are FULL of Faith and Of Holy Spirit.

In Jesus' Name, Amen†

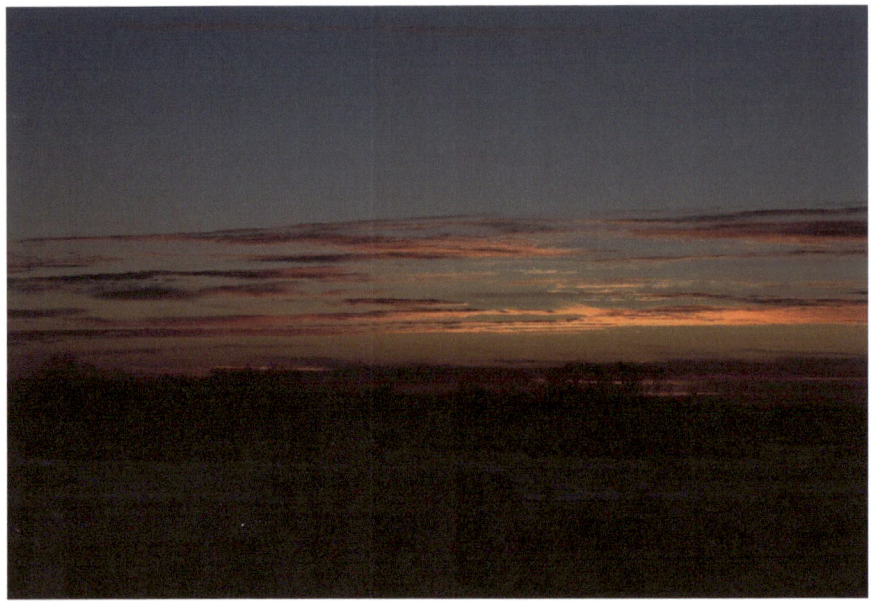

**Contentment**

Heavenly Father

Help me to keep my focus on You, regardless of what is going on around me. Help me to be content with what You have blessed me with. Help me to be content with what I have. Help me to be content and at peace with myself.

I choose to let go of anger, resentment, and frustration.
I choose to be happy, thankful, and glad.
I choose to celebrate YOU every day, by giving honor and glory to YOU.

In Jesus' Name, Amen†

**Wisdom**

Heavenly Father

Help me to see clearly and accept those whom YOU have chosen to be a part of my life and purpose. Give me the wisdom I need to lead as well as to follow, to produce the fruit that YOU have ordained for me. To recognize the things that I need to let go of, the things that are hindering me.
Give me YOUR peace that surpasses all understanding, so that no matter what YOU get The Glory.

In Jesus' Name, Amen†

**Vision**

Heavenly Father

Help me to NOT "see you in a box" based on my lack of knowledge of You. Help me to see YOU HIGH AND LIFTED UP, help me to see YOU as YOU ARE, Creator of Heaven and Earth, Creator of all living things, both small and great.

Help me to realize that I cannot contain YOU "in a box." Help me to STOP limiting what YOU are able to do in my life and those around me. YOU are all knowing, and all powerful, and there is NOTHING too hard for YOU. Help me, Father, to be faithful to YOU and trust YOU, even in my areas of doubt and unbelief.

In Jesus' Name, Amen†

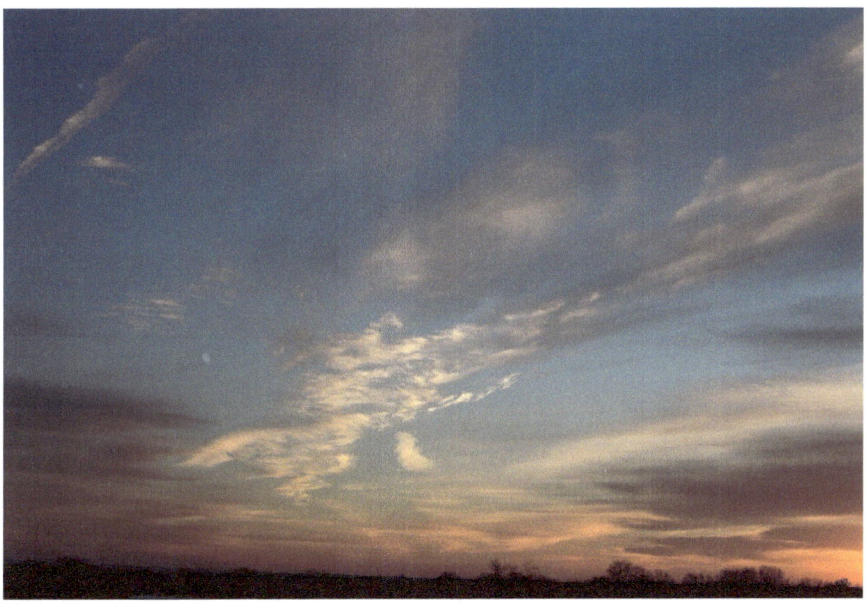

**Not MY Will but Yours**

Heavenly Father

Help me to make every effort to get understanding and wisdom regarding my life, my purpose and my calling. Help me to keep my "eyes" on You and Your Word, regardless of the distractions that come my way. Help me to remember that IN YOU, I live, move, and breathe. Help me to stay focused, just as Jesus remained focused as He said to You, "Nevertheless, NOT MY WILL BUT YOURS BE DONE."

Grant me the peace, stamina, and faith that it takes to STAND and not be moved.

Thank You in advance for all of these things.

In Jesus' Name, Amen†

**Comfort**

Heavenly Father

Comfort those who are hurting. Bring peace to those are in strife. Healing to those who are sick and oppressed. Deliverance to those who are bound. Unity to those who are divided. And restoration and salvation to the lost.

In Jesus' Name, Amen†

**Forgive us Lord**

Heavenly Father

Forgive us for our lack of love and unity. We can do nothing without others, and in order to do so, we must be in unity. We must show love towards one another.

You have already warned us in Your Word that there would be a lack of love and unity, yet instead of doing our part to show love and unity, we have allowed the lack of it to become more noticeable in our everyday interactions.

You tell us in Your Word to show ourselves to be friendly, to respect one another, to give honor to whom honor is due. Yet, instead, we murmur, complain, and backbite one another. We criticize and say disparaging things about others.

Forgive us, Lord. forgive me, Lord.

In Jesus' Name, Amen✝

**Wait on The Lord**

Heavenly Father

Help me to wait ON You. To WAIT on You for the answer, for the solution, for strength, for wisdom, for security, for blessings, for guidance, for peace, for joy, for EVERYTHING I have need of.
Help me to put my total TRUST in and ON You.

In Jesus' Name, Amen†

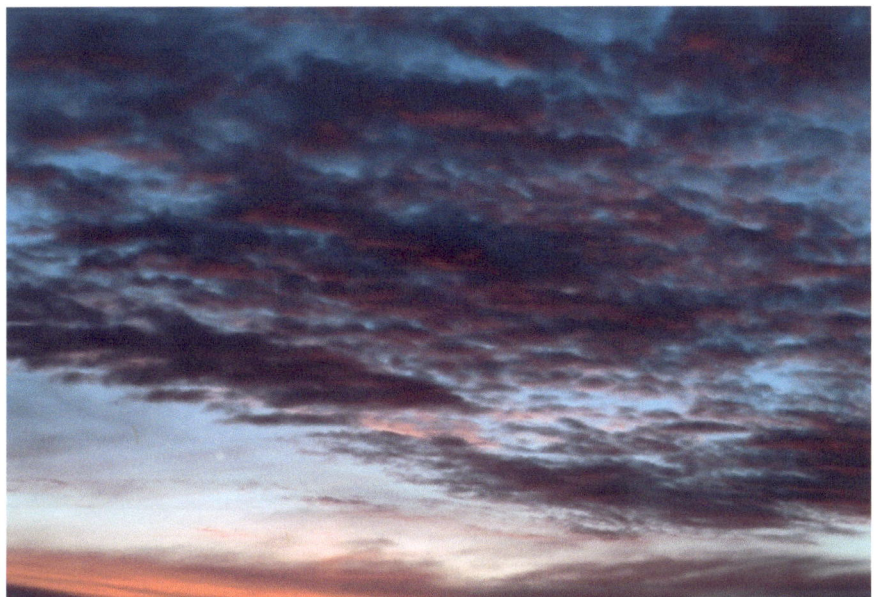

**Your Truth**

Heavenly Father

Reveal to us YOUR Truth through Your Word, by Your Holy Spirit so that we will not become deceived by simple words and demonic dreams. Help us to HEAR clearly what You are saying. Help us to be obedient to what You are saying to us. Help us to apply those things that You speak to our own lives FIRST, then share with others as You direct us to do so.

When You speak a Word of correction and rebuke, help us to ensure that we are LISTENING to YOUR voice, and not the voice of the stranger. Thank You in advance for giving us listening and attentive ears to what YOU are speaking.

In Jesus' Name, Amen†

## Comfort

Heavenly Father

Comfort the Mothers who have lost their children to death in the last few days. It is never easy for a parent to lose a child, regardless of the circumstance.

Lord, I pray that you give the parents peace and comfort as only YOU are able to do. Father, I especially pray for the Mothers of these children, as no mother ever expects to see their child pass before them, let alone as their life is just beginning.

We call on You, Prince of Peace, to provide comfort right Now.

In Jesus' Name, Amen†

"Children are a gift of the Lord, the fruit of the womb is a reward."
Psalm 127:3

## What Shall Separate Us?

Heavenly Father

Let there be nothing that separates me from Your love. Let nothing cause me to take my focus off of You. Let nothing hinder me from doing Your Will. Let nothing become more important than You in my life.

In Jesus' Name, Amen†

38 "For I am persuaded, that neither death, nor life, nor angels, nor principalities, nor powers, nor things present, nor things to come," 39 "Nor height, nor depth, nor any other creature, shall be able to separate us from the love of God, which is in Christ Jesus our Lord."
Romans 8:38-39

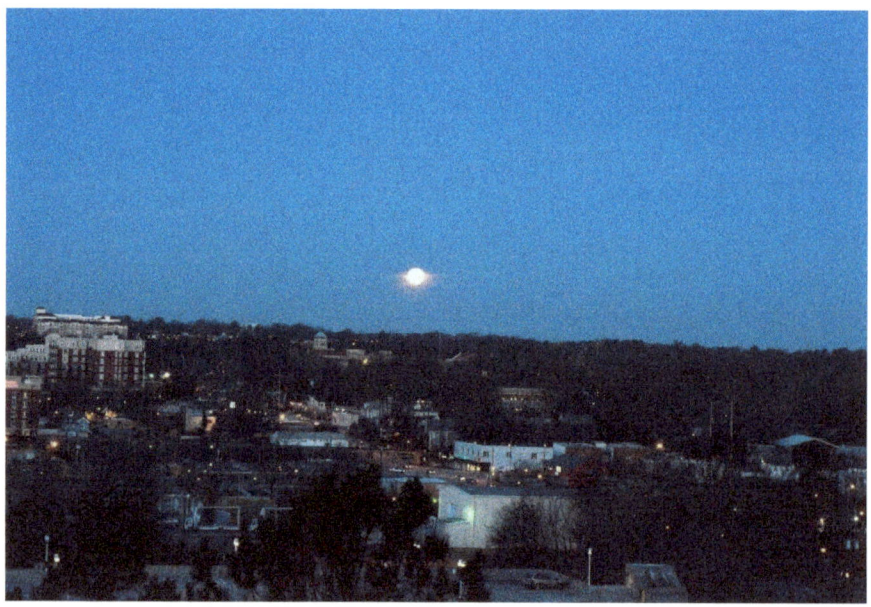

**The Love of Jesus**

Heavenly Father

I pray for YOUR guidance and wisdom regarding my interaction with everyone I come into contact with; Everyone, including my family, my co-workers, and strangers, that I meet.

May they all see YOU in me.
May they see and experience The Love of Jesus in and through me. Help me to remember that it is for YOUR glory, not my own, that I serve You. Thank you, Father, for YOUR peace that surpasses "all understanding." Thank YOU for producing the proper fruit in me.

In Jesus' Name, Amen†

"In your relationships with one another, have the same mindset as Christ Jesus."

Philippians 2:5

**My Focus**

Heavenly Father

May my worship and praise be OF and TO You and not the things and people around me. May my focus be ON and ABOUT You. May those who do not yet know You see YOU through me.

In Jesus' Name, Amen†

**Forgive Us Lord**

Heavenly Father

Forgive us for NOT following Your Word regarding judging others. Help us to remember that we ourselves, needed your Grace and Mercy, and we STILL need Your Grace and Mercy. Help us to remember that the way we judge others is HOW we will be judged.

Teach us HOW to judge THE WAY You instructed us to judge according to You Word. Forgive us for being prideful, and help us to be humble, so that when we do judge righteously, it will be done in love, and not in hate, or in pride or for revenge.

In Jesus' Name, Amen†

John 7:24

**Godly Example – True Man**

Heavenly Father

Thank You for the example of what it means to be a Godly Man. A man that seeks You and Worships You. Thank You for raising up a generation of Men whose desire and focus is to be obedient to You, Your Word, and Your Ways. To be a Man that takes responsibility for his actions, and truly loves his wife and family. To be a man of respect, honor, and integrity. Help us to train our children to be respectful of You, to know You, and to respect others.

May every boy on his way to manhood be taught and trained in Your Ways, for Your Glory. May every son of a single parent see and understand what it means to be a Man of Valor, a Man of God, A Husband, and Father. May every daughter of a single parent have clear vision and understanding of what a TRUE Man "looks like" according to Your Word.

In Jesus' Name, Amen†

## Godly Example – True Woman

Heavenly Father

Thank You for the example of what it means to be a Godly Woman. A woman that seeks You and Worships You. Thank You for raising up a generation of Women whose desire and focus is to be obedient to You, Your Word, and Your Ways. To be a Woman that takes responsibility for her actions, and truly loves her husband and family. To be a woman of respect, honor, and integrity. Help us to train our children to be respectful of You, to know You, and to respect others.

May every girl on her way to womanhood be taught and trained in Your Ways, for Your Glory. May every daughter of a single parent see and understand what it means to be a Woman of Valor, a Woman of God, A Wife, and Mother.

May every son of a single parent have clear vision and understanding of what a TRUE Woman "looks like" according to Your Word.

In Jesus' Name, Amen†


14 "A person will be satisfied with good by the fruit of his or her words, And the deeds of a person's hands will return to him or her." 15 "The way of a fool is right in their own eyes, but a wise person is one who listens to counsel."
Proverbs 12:14-15

## Glory to YOUR Name

Our Father in Heaven, Hallowed be Your name.
Your kingdom come. Your will be done, On earth as it is in heaven.
Give us this day our daily bread. And forgive us our debts,
As we forgive our debtors. And do not lead us into temptation,
But deliver us from the evil one.
For Yours is the kingdom and the power and the glory forever.

Amen†

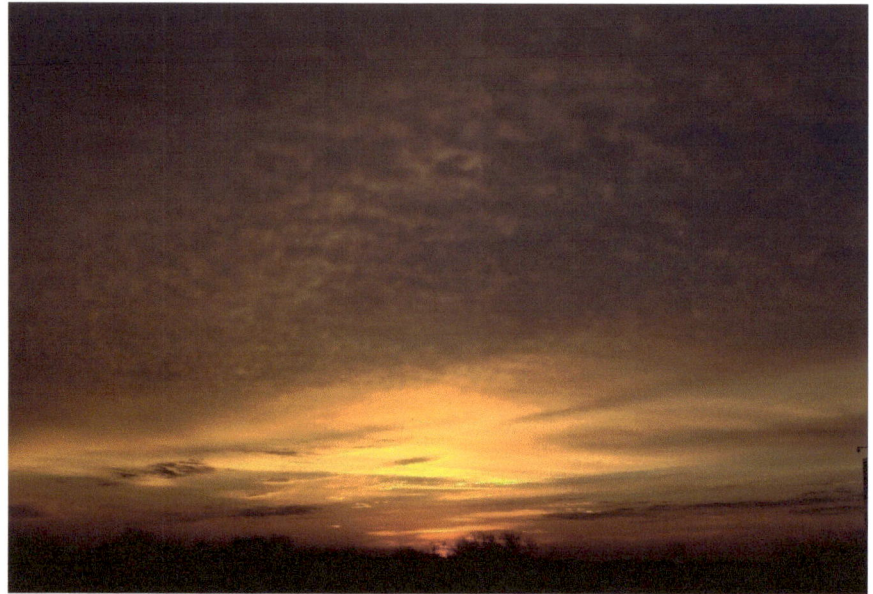

**I Praise You**

Heavenly Father

Please receive my Praise and Worship as an Offering to You. May I glorify You in all that you have done, are doing right now, and will do in the future. As I praise and worship You, help Me to truly do so with a pure heart, an honest heart, regardless of where I find myself, my Praise, and my Worship. Help me to glorify You.

In Jesus' Name, Amen†

**Redeemed**

Heavenly Father

Let each of us who claim The Name of Jesus, as Lord and Savior, truly be challenged by You and YOU alone to live according to "the gospel of Jesus." That "good news" of His Redemption and Love.

Let us be challenged to live by The Words of Jesus to love one another, to share His message to all that we meet, to work out our own soul salvation with proper respect of You.

Let us be challenged not to take it lightly, or as a game. Let us be challenged to show our Faith by our works, and not our works to be seen. Let us be challenged to Worship You in Spirit and In Truth.

In Jesus' Name, Amen†

**Lead us Lord**

Heavenly Father

Lead and guide us into all truth, so that we may live in peace with all mankind as You desire for us to do. Let us make YOU, and Your Son Jesus, known to everyone we come in contact with, through our humble heart and attitude. Not attempting to be better than the next person or to look down on the less fortunate.

Make us all vessels of honor for YOUR glory and not our own.

In Jesus' Name, Amen†

**Mercy**

Heavenly Father

Thank you for Your mercy. Thank you for building patience in me as YOU develop my faith and provide wisdom that comes from YOU and only from YOU.

In Jesus' Name, Amen†

2 "My brethren, count it all joy when ye fall into divers temptations;" 3 "Knowing this, that the trying of your faith worketh patience." 4 "But let patience have her perfect work, that ye may be perfect and entire, wanting nothing." 5 "If any of you lack wisdom, let him ask of God, that giveth to all men liberally, and upbraideth not; and it shall be given him." James 1:2-5

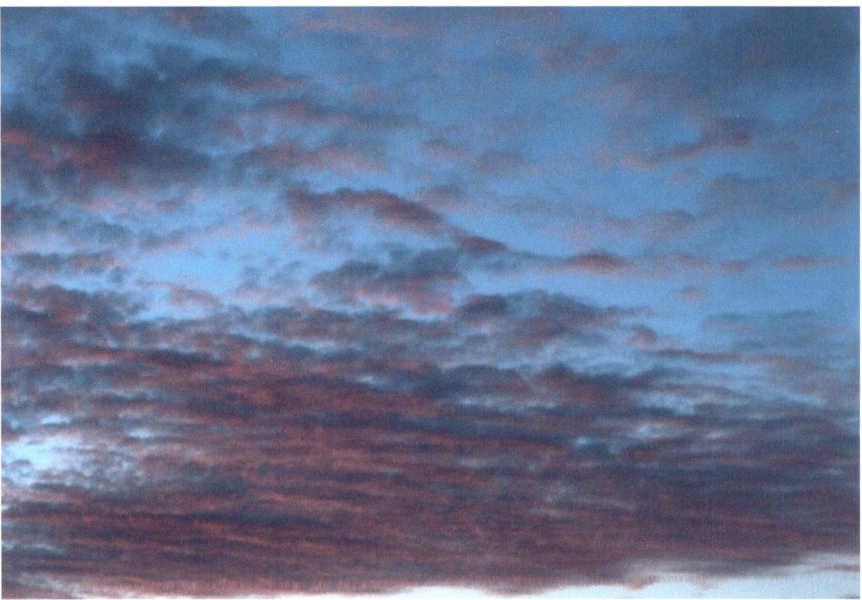

## Simplicity and Clarity

Heavenly Father

Thank you for the simplicity and clarity of Your Word. Help us to spend time reading and studying Your Word so that we will come to now TRUTH, and to have wisdom to know when Your Word is being misrepresented, misused, and misinterpreted.

Help us to know when Your Word is being used to manipulate us in to doing the opposite of what You have stated in Your Word.
Thank You for giving us TRUE teachers of Your Word who have Your Will in mind and no other hidden agenda or motive.

In Jesus' Name, Amen†

**Cast Your Cares**

Heavenly Father

Help me to cast my situation and circumstances up on to YOU instead of complaining and grumbling about it to others who either do not truly care or cannot or will not do anything to help or to be encouraging. Help Me to follow the example of King David, who encouraged HIMSELF IN The Lord, the example of Jesus who separated HIMSELF from others and the crowd, to spend time with YOU in Prayer, and as Paul the apostle and Silas, by singing songs to You, whether its hymns, Psalms, and/or spiritual songs. My "midnight" is not as dark as someone else's "midnight," so help me to be thankful IN all things because YOU care for Me.

In Jesus' Name, Amen†

"Casting all your care upon HIM; for he cares for you."
1 Peter 5:7

## Help Me Please YOU

Heavenly Father

Give me strength, clarity, and determination regarding the things YOU have placed in my charge to do. Help me to be concerned about pleasing YOU and not those around me. Help me to be obedient to what YOU ask of me, and not what others demand of me, or what I THINK should be done. Help me to do what YOU would have me to do, to the best of my ability without care or concern about what others say or think about it, as long as I am striving to do YOUR will in all I do.

In Jesus' Name, Amen†

**YOUR Will**

Heavenly Father

Help us to truly walk and live in unity according to Your Word, through and by Your Spirit, so that TRUE power from on High will always be made known to everyone we encounter.

May our presence change the atmosphere of our surroundings with Your Glory being released. May those who do not know you, see YOU in us, and cause a desire in them to WANT to know and serve You.

In Jesus' Name, Amen†

**Words of FIRE**

Heavenly Father

May the words that I speak be YOUR words of truth and wisdom, not my words in order to show that I know what I am talking about, or that I am right, or that I have it all together, and that my words are truth and wisdom for everyone to hear.

May I not speak having said nothing, but rather, help me to speak YOUR words, make them FIRE in my mouth. May the Fire of Your Presence Be In My speaking and not the wind, the words with no substance.
In Jesus' Name, Amen†

"The Lord GOD of Hosts says: Because you have spoken this word, I am going to make My words become fire in your mouth."
Jeremiah 5:14

**Priority ONE**

Heavenly Father

Help ME to make YOU, Father, Son, and Holy Spirit, my Number One Priority. Help me to focus my attention on and towards You before I "look" at my situation and my circumstances. They are changing, the will change, people in my life will change, but YOU Father, God, NEVER changes.
Thank you, Jesus, for being a "friend that sticks closer than a brother," a sister, a husband, or a wife. Show me how YOU would have ME to live my life for YOUR glory.

In Jesus' Name, Amen†

"For you have made the Lord, my refuge,
Even the Most High, your dwelling place.
No evil will befall you,
Nor will any plague come near your tent.
For He will give His angels charge concerning you,
To guard you in all your ways.
And let him see My salvation."
Psalm 91:9-11

**What Do You Do?**

What do you do when you have your trust and faith IN The Lord, yet tragedy still strikes?

What do you do when you just want to enjoy time with friends and family yet there is always some hindrance, some sort of distraction?
What do You do?

Heavenly Father

We acknowledge that we need YOU now more than ever. Father, we are reminded that YOU said "these things must come, but FEAR NOT."
Lord, help us all to walk in love. Live in love. To enjoy our lives as best we can WITHOUT being fearful of what may come. YOU are our "place of Safety."

Help us to stand firm in YOU. Help us to remember that YOU do have "Angels Watching Over Us." Help us to be mindful that even as we have begun a new day, that tomorrow is still NOT promised to us.
Give us a heart of compassion for those who are suffering. No matter the reason for that suffering, help us to show YOUR LOVE. Father, give peace and comfort to all of those who are grieving at this very moment due to the untimely death of a loved one, regardless of how it happened.
We look to YOU for our Safety, our Strength, and our Direction for today and for the future.

In Jesus' Name, Amen†

## Cancel the Noise

Being stuck in a rut is like being placed into a coffin while alive. Feelings of despair, anguish, low self-esteem, and a lack of passion develops. The gifts and talents that are embedded in your DNA become dormant, stagnate. You begin to question:

"Why am I really here?"
"Does it really matter?"

It's time to CANCEL THE NOISE. It's time to DO and BE who and what God, The Creator of ALL Creation, has created us to do and be. Stop listening to the negative, doubtful, hateful "voices."
CANCEL THAT NOISE and listen to The Voice of The Creator.

Heavenly Father

Thank You for a brand-new day.
Forgive me for allowing myself to be placed in a box that You never intended for me to be in. Help me to use my gifts and talents to be a blessing to others as well as MYSELF. Help me to see clearly that I AM worthy to enjoy blessings, love, and peace because YOU designed it for us all.

Help me to cancel the noise and the voice of the enemy. Help me to hear YOU clearly in and for every area of my life. Give me the mental strength and physical stamina I need to keep moving forward. I declare that starting NOW, I will no longer "walk and live" in a rut.

THANK YOU, Father, for taking me out of that dead place and into a place of life, love, and peace.

Thank You for showing me who I AM so that others can see who THEY ARE. Thank You for helping me CANCEL THE NOISE.

In Jesus' Name, Amen†

**Voice of Understanding**

Heavenly Father

Thank you for the RIGHT words to speak today and every day. Help me to always do what is right and pleasing to You and not to others. And lead me to those who will give me proper counsel and correct me when I need it most.

In Jesus' Name, Amen†

1 "My son, if you will receive my words And treasure my commandments within you," 2 "Make your ear attentive to wisdom, Incline your heart to understanding;" 3 "For if you cry for discernment, Lift your voice for understanding;" 4 "If you seek her as silver And search for her as for hidden treasures;" 5 "Then you will discern the fear of the LORD And discover the knowledge of God."
Proverbs 2:1-5

## All Truth

Heavenly Father

Thank You for leading and guiding me into ALL truth and wisdom so that I may truly understand and have proper respect for You. Lord may my respect for You be seen by You in everything I hear, do, and say.
Help me to search for wisdom in the hidden things that lead me to You.

In Jesus' Name, Amen†

**Offending God**

Is that even possible?

Think very carefully before answering that question. Often, we think of offense as a wrong done to us or against us. A harsh word or other type of attack against someone. Or, a crime that is committed. But what about offending God?

Offending God comes when we, you and I, do what is contrary to His Word. By missing the mark, which is a nice way of saying "sin." That is how you and I offend God. By our sin. Now, here is the beautiful thing about offending God: HE has already forgiven us for those offenses and gives us the chance to "get it right." He clearly states to us, "Go and sin no more." Let's do our best to "go and sin no more" and allow HIM to clean us of all impurities, and yes, our sins, so that we have God's Face Shining Upon us. He will not turn His back to us.

Heavenly Father

Forgive us for the ways we have offended You. Forgive us of all sin. One sin is not worse than another. ALL sin is sin in Your eyes. Help us to live our lives in a way that brings Glory to YOU just as Jesus' life, death, and resurrection Glorified YOU.

Help us to see our sins as sins and not excuses. Help us to renew our thinking, to renew our minds with Your Word.
Thank You, Heavenly Father, for a second chance, even if it's second chance number 100. May I NOT be one that offends anyone, especially YOU, Father. THANK You, Father, for Your Grace and for Your Mercy.

In Jesus' Name, Amen†

Psalm 51
Matthew 18:7
Romans 8

## Be Amazed

Believe for the Impossible to BE Possible. Be AMAZED at what God has in store. He has already given us The Promises. It is up to you and I to believe, to receive it.

Heavenly Father

THANK YOU for YOUR promises to ME. Not only to me, but to my family and others who love and serve YOU.

Help us to remain faithful to what YOU have given us to do. What YOU have called us to. Give us wisdom to serve others with a joyful, loving heart. Give us BOLD FAITH and Tenacity to Believe the Impossible to BE Possible because YOU said it would happen. Forgive us for our unbelief even as we say we believe.

Open our "eyes" that we may see and open our "ears" that we may hear what YOU are showing and speaking to us. Father, I thank YOU and praise YOU for what YOU are about to do.

In Jesus' Name, Amen†

"Look around you... and SEE! Be astonished (amazed, in awe)! For I WILL WORK A WORK In Your Days... Says The Lord."
Habukkuk 1:5

**Majestic**

Heavenly Father
Thank you for this majestic time with you.
In Jesus' Name, Amen†

"Lord, Our Lord, How MAJESTIC is YOUR Name in ALL the earth."
Psalm 8:9

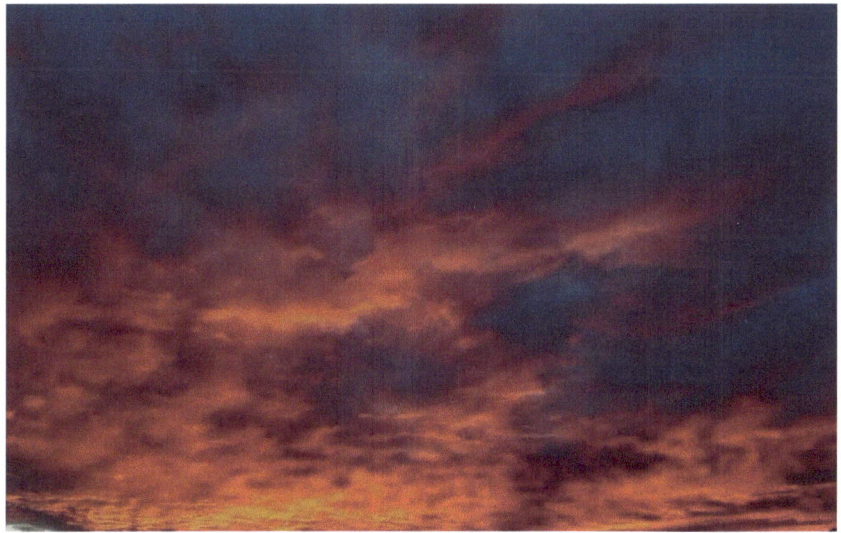

# Index

Action Pg 25
All Truth Pg 74
Armor of God Ephes. 6:11 Pg 9
Be Amazed Habukkuk 1:5 Pg 76
Boldness in Truth: 2 Peter 1 Pg 19
Calm Psalm 34 Pg 18
Cancel The Noise Pg 72
Cast Your Cares 1 Peter 5:7 Pg 66
Comfort Pg 49
Comfort Psalm 127:3 Pg 53
Contentment Pg 45
Determination Pg 10
Faith: Hebrews 11:1-6 Pg 2
Focus Mark 14:26-31 Pg 38
Forgive Us Lord John 7:24 Pg 57
Forgive Us Lord Pg 50
Forgive Romans 8:1-39 Pg 35
Gifts and Talents Pg 7
Glory Pg 43
Glory to YOUR Name Pg 60
God Loves ME in Spite of Me: Psalm 31:7 Pg 29
God's Promises Mark 9:24 Pg 11
Godly Example-True Man Pg 58
Godly Example-True Woman Proverbs 12:14-15 Pg 59
Help Me Please You Pg 67
Honor Pg 26
Honoring God: Proverbs 16:1-33 Pg 8
How to Pray 2 Chronicles 7:14 Pg 21
Humility Psalm 51; Romans 3:10; Matthew 23; Romans 2:17-24 Pg 40
Humility Ecclesiastes 12:13-14 Pg 6
I Praise You Pg 61
Insight Pg 13
Lead Us Lord Pg 63
Let Your Glory Rise Pg 33
Love Pg 20
Majestic Psalm 8:9 Pg 77
Mercy James 1:2-5 Pg 64
My Focus Pg 56
My Safe Place Psalm 91:2 Pg 37
Not MY Will But Yours Pg 48
Not My Will Pg 27
Offending God Psalm 51; Matthew 18:7; Romans 8 Pg 75
Peace Pg 15
Prayer of Deliverance Psalm 31:1-5 Pg 36
PriorityONE Psalm 91:1-11 Pg 70
Priority Pg 28
Protection and Guidance Pg 32
Provision Philippians 3:1 Pg 31
Purpose John 6:27-29 Pg 4
Redeemed Pg 62
Seasons Genesis 8:22; Jeremiah 29:11; Rom. 8 Pg 41
Seeking HIM Pg 44
Service Pg 14
Shalom (Peace) Pg 42
Simplicity and Clarity Pg 65
Son of God Hebrews 10:12 Pg 3
Storm of Life Psalm 91 Pg 30
Thank You Pg 16
The Gift of Wisdom Pg 34
The Love of Jesus Philippians 2:5 Pg 55
Trust Pg 17
Vision Pg 47
Voice of Understanding Proverbs 2:1-5 Pg 73
Wait On The Lord Pg 51
What Do You Do? Pg 71
What Shall Separate Us? Romans 8:38-39 Pg 54
Whom Shall I Fear? Psalm 27:1-6 Pg 39
Why? Pg 22
Wisdom Pg 12
Wisdom Pg 46
Wisdom Pg 5
Words of Fire Jerem.5:14 Pg 69
You Have Control, Lord Pg 23
Your Truth Pg 52
Your Will Pg 68
Your Wisdom Pg 24

## About The Author

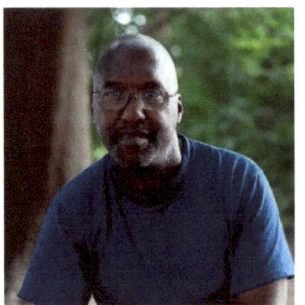

Roger D. King is a Freelance Photographer, Speaker and Writer specializing in motivating and encouraging others to discover and follow their God-given purpose and dreams.

He has also been involved in Prophetic Ministry for 20 years and currently resides in Raleigh, North Carolina.

For more information visit www.rogerdking.com

**Roger D. King**

**PO Box 28476**

**Raleigh, NC 27611-28476**

"Majestic" An Affirmation Media, LLC Project in cooperation with Empowerment Media and Publishing.

Editing Services Provided by Bonniejean Alford. As a writer, editor, and identity strategist with two Master of Art degrees (Sociology and Communication), she provides a variety of specialty communication services aimed at enhancing quality brand messaging. Visit her company website at www.alfordenterprises.net

www.ingramcontent.com/pod-product-compliance
Lightning Source LLC
Chambersburg PA
CBHW040224220526
45473CB00001B/107